A Discourse of Trade
Nicholas Barbon

Prism Key Press, 2013.
New York, NY.

www.PrismKeyPress.com

ISBN-13: 978-1490935645
ISBN-10: 1490935649

A Discourse of Trade

Nicholas Barbon

Table of Contents

Table of Contents

The Preface

The Greatness and Riches of the United Provinces, and States of Venice, consider'd, with the little Tract of Ground that belongs to either of their Territories, sufficiently Demonstrate the great Advantage and Profit that Trade brings to a Nation.

And since the Old Ammunition and Artillery of the Grecians and Romans are grown out of Use; such as Stones, Bows, Arrows, and battering Rams, with other Wooden Engines, which were in all Places easily procured or made: And the Invention of Gunpowder hath introduced another sort of Ammunition and Artillery, whose Materials are made of Minerals, that are not to be found in all Countries; such as Iron, Brass, Lead, Salt-petre, and Brimstone; and therefore where they are wanting, must be procured by Traffick. Trade is now become as necessary to Preserve Governments, as it is useful to make them Rich.

And notwithstanding the great Influence, that Trade now hath in the Support and Welfare of States and Kingdoms, yet there is nothing more unknown, or that Men differ more in their Sentiments, than about the True Causes that raise and promote Trade.

Livy, and those Antient Writers, whose elevated Genius set them upon the Inquiries into the Causes of the Rise and Fall of governments, have been very exact in describing the several Forms of Military Discipline, but take no Notice of Trade; and Machiavel a Modern Writer, and the best, though he lived in a Government, where the Family of Medicis had advanced themselves to the Soveraignty by their riches, acquired by Merchandizing, doth not mention Trade, as any way interested in the Affairs of State.

Of Trade and the Stock, or Wares of Trade

Trade is the Making, and Selling of one sort of Goods for another; The making is called Handy-Craft Trade, and the maker an Artificer; The Selling is called Merchandizing, and the Seller a Merchant: The Artificer is called by several Names from the sort of goods he makes. As a Clothier, Silk-weaver, Shoo-maker, or Hatter, etc. from Making of Cloth, Silk, Shooes, or Hats; and the Merchant is distinguished by the Names of the Countrey he deals to, and is called, Dutch, French, Spanish or Turkey Merchant.

The chief End or Business of Trade, is to make a profitable Bargain: In making of a Bargain there are these things to be considered; The Wares to be Sold, the Quantity and Quality of those Wares, the Value or Price of them, the Money or Credit, by which the Wares are bought, the Interest that relates to the time of performing the Bargain.

The Stock and Wares of all Trades are the Animals, Vegitables, and Minerals of the whole Universe, whatsoever the Land or Sea produceth. These Wares may be divided into Natural and Artificial; Natural Wares are those which are sold as Nature Produceth them; As Flesh, Fish, and Fruits, etc. Articifial Wares are those which by Art are Changed into another Form than Nature gave them; As Cloth, Calicoes, and wrought Silks, etc. which are made of Wool, Flax, Cotten, and Raw Silks.

Both these Sorts of Wares are called the Staple Commoditys of those Countreys where they chiefly abound, or are made. There are Different Climates of the Heavens, some very Hot, some very Cold, other Temperate; these Different Climates produce Different Animals, Vegitables, & Minerals. The Staples of the hot Country are Spices; the Staples of the

Cold, Furrs; but the more Temperate Climates produce much the same sorts of Commoditys; but by difference of the Quality or Conveniency of place where they abound, the become the Staple of each Country, whre they are either best or easier acquired or exchanged: Thus, Herrings, and other Fish are the Staples of Holland; the Dutch living amongst the Water, are most naturally inclined to Fishing: English Wool being the best in the World, is the Staple of England, for the same reason. Oyles of Italy, Fruits of Spain, Wine of France, with several other sorts of Commoditys, are the Staples of their several Countrys.

Staple Commodities may be divided into Native or Forreign; the Native Staple is what Each Country doth Naturally and best produce; Forreign Staple, any Forreign Commodity, which a Country acquires by the sole Trade to a Forreign Place, or sole possession of a particular Art; as Spices are the Staple of Holland; and the making of Glass and Paper, were the Staple of Venice.

From the Stock, or Wares of Trade, these Three Things are Observable:

1. The Native Staple of each Country is the Riches of the Country, and is perpetual, and never to be consumed; Beasts of the Earth, Fowls of the Air, and Fishes of the Sea, Naturally Increase: There is Every Year a New Spring and Autumn, which produceth a New Stock of Plants and Fruits. And the Minerals of the Earth are Unexhaustable; and if the Natural Stock be Infinite, the Artificial Stock that is made of the Natural, must be Infinite, as Woollen and Linnen Cloth, Calicoes, and wrought Silk, which are made of Flax, Wool, Cotton, and Raw Silks.

This sheweth a Mistake of Mr Munn, in his Discourse of Trade, who commends Parsimony, Frugality, and Sumptuary Laws, as the means to make a Nation Rich; and uses an Argument, from a Simile, supposing a Man to have 1000 l. per annum, and 2000 l. in a Chest, and spends Yearly 1500 l. per annum, he will in four Years time Waste his 2000 l. This is true, of a Person, but not of a Nation; because his Estate is finite, but the Stock of a Nation Infinite, and can never be consumed; For what is Infinite, can neither receive Addition by Parsimony, nor suffer Diminution, by Prodigality.

2. The Native Staple of Each Contry, is the Foundation of it's Forreign Trade: And no Nation have any Forreign Commodities, but what are at firs brought in by the Exchange of the Native; for at the beginning of Forreign Trade, a Nation hath nothing else to Exchange; The Silver & Gold from Spain; the Silks from Turkey, Oyls from Italy, wine from France, and all other Forreign Goods are brought into England, by the Exchange of the English Cloth, or some other Staple of England.

3. That Forreign Staples are uncertain Wealth: Some Countries by the Sole Trade to another Country, or by the Sole Possession of some Arts, gain a Staple of Forreign Commodities, which may be as profitable as the Native, so long as they enjoy the Sole possession of that Trade or Art. But that is uncertain; for other Nations find out the way of Trading to the same place: the Artists for Advantage, Travel into other Countries, and the Arts are discover'd. Thus Portugal had the Sole Trade of India; afterwards the Venetians got a great Share of the Trade, and now the Dutch and English, have a greater share than both: The Arts of making several sorts of Silks, were chiefly confined to Genoa, & Naples; afterward Travelled into France, since into England and Holland, and are now Practised there in as great perfection as they were in Italy; So have other Arts wander'd, as the making of Looking-Glasses from Venice into England, the making of Paper from Venice into France and Holland.

11

Of the Quantity and Quality of Wares

The Quantity of all Wares are known by Weight or Measure. The Reason of Gravity is not understood, neither is it Material to this Purpose; Whether is proceeds from the Elastisity of Air, or Weight of the utmost Spheer, or from what other Causes, its sufficient, that the ways of Trying the Weights of Bodies are perfectly discover'd by the Ballance. There are Two Sorts of Weights in Common Use, the Troy, and Averdupois.

The First are used to Weigh Goods of most Value, as Gold, Silver and Silk, etc. The Latter for Coarser, and more Bulky Goods, as Lead, Iron, etc.

There are Two Sorts of Measures, the one for Fluid Bodies, a the Bushel, Gallon and Quart, for Measuring Corn, Wine and Oyl; the other for the Measuring the Dimensions of Solid Bodies, as a Yard, Ell, etc. to Measure Cloth, Silk, etc.

The Weights and Measures of all Countries differs, but that is no Prejudice to Trade; they are all made certain by the Custom or Laws of the Place,and the Trader knows the Weight or Measure in Use, in the Place he Deals to. It is the Care of the government, to prevent and punish the Fraud of False Weights and Measures, and in most Trading- Cities, there are Publick Weigh-Houses, and Measures: The Fraud of the Ballance, which is from the unequal Length of the end of the Beam, is least perceivable; and therefore in Weighing Goods of Value, they usually Weigh them in both Scales.

The Qualities of Wares are known by their Colour, sound, Smell, Taste, Make, or Shape.

The Difference in the Qualities of Wares are very difficultly distinguished; those Organs that are the proper Judges of those Differencies, do very much disagree; some Men have clearer Eyes, some more distinguishing Ears, and other nicer Noses and Tastes; and every Man ahving a good Opinion of his own Faculties, it is hard to find a Judge to determine which is best: Besides, those Qualites that belong to Artificial Wares,such as depend upon the Mixture, Make or Shape of them, are more difficultly discover'd: Those Wares, whose Quality are produced by the just Mixture of different Bodies, such as Knives and Razors, whose sharpness arise from the Good Temperament and Mixture of the Steel & Iron, are not to be found out, but by the Use of them: And so doth the Mixture, and well making of Hats, Cloth, and many other things.

Because the Difference in the Qualities of Wares, ae so difficultly understood, it is that the Trader serves an Apprendiceship to learn them; and the Knowledge of them is called the Mystery of Trade; and in common Dealing, the Buyer is forced to rely on the Skill and Honesty of the Seller, to deliver Wares with such Qualities as he affirms them to have: It is the Sellers Interest, from the Expectation of further Dealing, not to deceive; because his Shop, the Place of Dealing, is known: Therefore, those Persons that buy of Pedlars, and Wandering People, run Great Hazard of being Cheated.

Those Wares, whose Chief Qualities consist in Shape, such as all Wearing Apparel, do not so much depend uon the Honesty of the Seller; for tho' the Trader or Maker, is the Inventor of the Shape, yet it is the Fancy and Approbation of the Buyer, that brings it into Use, and makes it pass for a Fashion.

Of the Value and Price of Wares

The Value of all Wares arise from their Use; Things of no Use, have no Value, as the English Phrase is, They are good for nothing.

The Use of Things, are to supply the Wants and Necessities of Man: There are Two General Wants that Mankind is born with; the Wants of the Body,a nd the Wants of the Mind; To supply these two Necessities, all things under the Sun become useful, and therefore have a Value.

Wares, useful to supply the Wants of the Body, are all things necessary to support Life, such are in Common Estimation; all those Goods which are useful to supply the Three General Necessities of Man, Food, Clothes and Lodging; But if strictly Examined, nothing is absolutely necessary to support Life, but Food; for a great Part of Mankind go Naked, and lye in Huts and Caves; so that there are but few things that are absolutely necessary to supply the Wants of the Body.

Wares, that have their Value from supplying the Wants of the Mind, are all such things that can satisfie Desire; Desire implys Want: It is the Appetite of the Soul, and is as natural to the Soul, as Hunger to the Body.

The Wants of the Mind are infinite, Man naturally Aspires, and as his Mind is elevated, his Senses grow more refined, and more capable of Delight; his Desires are inlarged, and his Wants increase with his Wishes, which is for every thing that is rare, can gratifie his Senses, adorn his Body, and promote the Ease, Pleasure, and Pomp of Life.

Amongst the great Variety of things to satisfie the Wants of the Mind, those that adorn Mans Body, and advance the Pomp of Life, have the most general Use, and in all Ages, and amongst all sorts of Mankind, have been of Value.

The first Effects that the Fruit of the Tree of Knowledge

wrought upon the Parents of Mankind, was to make them cloath themselves, and it has made the most Visible Distinction of the Race, from the rest of the Creation: It is that by which his Posterity may write Man, for no Creatures adorn the Body but Man: Beside, the decking of the Body, doth not onely distinguish Man from Beast, but is the Mark of Difference and Superiority betwixt Man and Man.

There was never any part of Mankind so wild and barbarous, but they had Difference and Degree of Men amongst them, and invented some things to shew that Distinction.

Those that Cloathed with Skins, wore the Skins of those Beasts that are most difficultly taken; thus Hercules wore a Lyons Skin; and the Ermins and Sable, are still Badges of Honour. The Degree of Quality amongst the Affricans, is known by the waste Cloth, and amongst those that go naked, by adorning their Bodies with Colours, most rare amongst them, as the Red was the Colour most in Esteem amongst the Ancient Britains.

And the most Ancient and best of Histories, the Bible, shews, That amongst the Civilized People of the World, Ear-Rings, Bracelets, Hoods and Vails, with Changeable Suits of Apparel, were then worn: And the same Ornaments for the Body are still, and ever since have been Worn, only differing in Shapes and Fashions, according to the Custom of the Country.

The Shapes of Habits are much in use, to denote the Qualities of several men; but things rare and difficult to be obtained, are General Badges of Honour: From this Use, Pearls, Diamonds, and Precious Stones, have their Value: Things Rare are proper Ensigns of Honour, because it is Honourable to acquire Things Difficult.

The Price of Wares is the present Value; And ariseth by Computing the occasions or use for them, with the Quantity to serve that Occasion; for the Value of things depending on the use of them, the Over-pluss of Those Wares, which are more than can be used, become worth nothing; So that Plenty, in respect of the occasion, makes things cheap; and Scarcity, dear.

There is no fixt Price or Value of any thing for the Wares of Trades; The Animals and Vegetables of the Earth, depend on the Influence of Heaven, which sometimes causes Murrains, Dearth, Famine, and sometimes Years of great Plenty; therefore, the Value of things must accordingly Alter. Besides, the Use of most things being to supply the Wants of the Mind, and not the Necessitys of the Body; and those Wants, most of them proceeding from imagination, the Mind Changeth; the things grow out of Use, and so lose their Value.

There are two ways by which the value of things are a little guessed at; by the Price of the Merchant, and the Price of the Artificer: The Price that the Merchant sets upon his Wares, is by reckoning Prime Cost, Charges and Interest.

The Price of the Artificer, is by reckoning the Cost of the Materials,with the time of working them; The Price of Time is according to the Value of the Art, and the Skill of the Artist. Some Artificiers Reckon Twelve, others Fifteen, and some Twenty, and Thirty Shillings per Week.

Interest is the Rule that the Merchant Trades by; And Time, the Artificer, By which they cast up Profit, and Loss; for if the Price of their Wares, so alter either by Plenty, or by Change of the Use, that they do not pay the Merchant Interest, nor the Artificer for his Time, they both reckon they lose by their Trade.

But the Market is the best Judge of Value; for by the Concourse of Buyers and Sellers, the Quantity of Wares, and the Occasion for them are Best known: Things are just worth so much, as they can be sold for, according to the Old Rule, Valet Quantum Vendi potest.

Of Money, Credit and Interest

Mony is a Value made by a Law; and the Difference of its Value is known by the Stamp,and Size of the Piece. One Use of Mony is, It is the Measure of Value, by which the Value of all other things are reckoned; as when the Value of any thing is expressed, its said, It's worth so many shillings, or so many Pounds: Another Use of Mony is; It is a Change or Pawn for the Value of all other Things: For this Reason, the Value of Mony must be made certain by Law, or else it could not be made a certain Measure, nor an Exchange for the Value of all things.

It is not absolutely necessary, Mony should be made of Gold or Silver; for having its sole Value from the Law, it is not Material upon what Metal the Stamp be set. Mony hath the same Value, and performs the same Uses, if it be made of Brass, Copper, Tin, or any thing else. The Brass Mony of Spain, the Copper Mony of Sweeden, and Tin Farthings of England, have the same Value in Exchange, according to the Rate they are set at and perform the same Uses, to Cast up the Value of things, as the Gold and Silver Mony does; Six Pence in Farthings will buy the same thing as Six Pence in Silver; and the Value of a thing is well understood by saying, It is worth Eight Farthings, as that it is worth Two Pence: Gold and Silver, as well as Brass, Copper and Tin Mony, change their Value in those Countries, where the Law has no force, and yield no more than the Price of the Metal that bears the Stamp: Therefore, all Foreign Coins go by Weight, and are of no certain Value, but rise and fall with the Price of the metal. Pieces of Eight, yield sometimes 4 sh. 6 d. 4 sh. 7 d. and 4 sh 8 d. as the Value of Silver is higher or lower: And so doth Dollars, and all Forreign Coin, change their Value; and were it not for the Law that fixeth the Value, an English Crown Piece would now yield five Shillings and Two Pence, for so much is the Value of it, if it were melted, or in a Foreign Country. But the chief Advantage of making Silver and Gold, being Metals of great Value, those who design Profit by Counterfeiting the Coin, must Counterfeit the Metals, as well as the Stamp, which is more difficult than the Stamp. There's another Benefit to the Merchant, by such Mony; for Gold and Silver being Commodities for other Uses, than to make Mony; to make Plate, Gold & Silver Lace, Silks, etc. And Coins of little bulk, in respect of their Value, the Merchant transmits such Mony from Place to Place, in Specie, according as he finds his advantage, by the Rise of Bulloin; though this may be a Conveniency to the Merchant, it often proves a Prejudice to the State, by making Mony scarce: Therefore, there are Laws in most Countries, that Prohibit the Transportation of Mony, yet it cannot be prevented; for in Spain, though it be Capital, yet in Two Months after the Gallions are come home, there is scarce any Silver Mony to be seen in the Country.

Some Men have so great an Esteem for Gold and Silver, that they believe that they have an intrinsick Value in themselves, and cast up the value of every thing by them: The Reason of the Mistake, is, Because Mony being made of Gold and Silver, they do not distinguish betwixt Mony, and Gold and Silver. Mony hath a certain Value, because of the Law; but the Value of Gold and Silver are uncertain, and varies their Price, as much as Copper, Lead, or other Metals: And in the Places where they are dug, considering the smalness of their Veins,

with the Charges of getting them, they do not yield much more Profit than other Minerals, nor pay the Miners better Wages for digging them.

And were it not for the Waste, made of Gold and Silver, by Plate, Lace, Silks, and Guilding, and the Custom of the Eastern Princes, to lay them up and bury them, that Half which is dug in the West, is buried in the East. The great quantities dug out of the Earth, since the Discovery of the West Indies, would have so much lessened the Value, that by this time, they would not have much exceeded the Value of Tin, or Copper: Therefore, How greatly would those Gentlemen be disappointed, that are searching after the Philosopher's Stone, if they should at last happen to find it? For, if they should make but so great a Quantity of Gold and Silver, as they, and their Predecessors have spent in search after it, it would so alter, and bring down the Price of those Metals, that it might be a Question, whether they would get so much Over-plus by it, as would pay for the Metal they change into Gold and Silver. It is only the Scarcity that keeps up the Value, and not any Intrinsick Vertue or Quality in the Metals; For if the Vertue were to be considered, the Affrican that gives Gold for Knives, and Things made of Iron being a much more Useful metal, than either Gold or Silver. To Conclude this Objection, Nothing in it self hath a certain Value; One thing is as much worth as another: And it is time, and place, that give a difference to the Value of all things.

Credit is a Value raised by Opinion, it buys Goods as Mony doe's; and in all Trading Citys, there's more Wares sold upon Credit, then for present Mony.

There are Two Sorts of Credit; the one, is Grounded upon the Ability of the Buyer; the other, upon the Honesty: The first is called a Good man, which implys an Able Man; he generally buys upon short Time; to pay in a Month, which is accounted as ready Mony, and the Price is made accordingly. The other is accounted and Honest Man; He may be poor; he Generally buys for three and Six Months or longer so as to pay the Merchant by the Return of his own Goods; and therefore, the Seller relys more upon the Honesty of the Buyer, than his Ability: Most of the Retail Traders buy upon this Sort of Credit, and are usually Trusted for more than double they are worth.

In Citys of great Trade, there are publick Banks of Credit, as at Amsterdam and Venice: They are of great Advantage to Trade, for they make Payments easie, by preventing the Continual Trouble of telling over Mony, and cause a great Dispatch in Business: Publick Banks are of so great a Concern in Trade, that the Merchants of London, for want of such a Bank, have been forced to Carry their Cash to

Goldsmiths, and have thereby Raised such a Credit upon Goldsmiths Notes, that they pass in Payments from one to another like Notes upon the Bank; And although by this way of Credit, there hath been very Vast Sums of Mony lost, not less then too Millions within five and Twenty Years, yet the Dispatch and Ease in Trade is so great by such Notes, that the Credit is still in some Measure kept up.

Therefore, it is much to be wondered at, that since the City of London is the Largest, Richest, and Chiefest City in the World, for Trade; Since there is so much Ease, Dispatch, and Safety in a Publick Bank; and since such vast Losses has Happened for want of it; That the Merchant and Traders of London have not long before this time Addressed themselves, to the Government, for the Establishing of a Publick Bank.

The Common Objection, that a Publick Bank cannot be safe in a Monarchy, is not worth the Answering; As if Princes were not Governed by the same Rules of Policy, as States are, To do all things for the Well-fair of the Subjects, wherein their own Interest is concerned.

It is True, in a Government wholly Dispotical, whose Support is altogether in it's Millitary Forces; where Trade hath no Concern in the Affaires of the State; Brings no Revenue, There might be a Jealousy, that such a Bank might tempt a Prince to Seize it; when by doing it, he doth not Prejudice the Affairs of his Government: But in England, where the Government is not Dispotical; but the People Free; and have as great a Share in the soveraign Legislative Power, as the Subjects of any States have, or ever had; where the Customs makes great Figures, in the Kings Exchequer; where Ships are the Bullworks of the Kingdom; and where the Flourish of Trade is as much the Interest of the King as of the People, There can be no such Cause of Fear: For, What Objections can any Man make, that his Mony in the Bank, may not be as well secured by a Law, as his Property is? Or; Why he should be more afraid of Losing his Mony, than his Land or Goods?

Interest is the Rent of Stock, and is the same as the Rent of Land: The First, is the Rent of the Wrought or Artificial Stock; the latter, of the Unwrought or Natural Stock.

Interest is commonly reckoned for Mony; because the Mony borrowed at Interest, is to be repayed in Mony; but this is a mistake; For the Interest is paid for Stock: for the Mony borrowed, is laid out to buy Goods, or pay for them before bought: No Man takes up Mony at Interest, to lay it by him, and lose the Interest of it.

One use of Interest: It is the Rule by which the Trader makes up the Account of Profit and Loss; The Merchant expects by Dealing, to get more then Interest by his Goods; because of bad Debts, and other Hazards which he runs; and therefore, reckons all he gets above Interest, is Gain; all under, Loss; but if no more than Interest, neither Profit, nor Loss.

Another use of Interest, is, It is the measure of the Value of the Rent of Land; it sets the Price in Buying and Selling of Land: For, by adding three Years Interest more than is in the Principle, Makes the usual Value of the Land of the Country; The difference of three Year is allowed; Because Land is more certain than Mony or Stock. Thus in Holland, where Mony is at three per cent by reckoning how many times three is in a Hundred Pounds, which is Thirty Three; and Adding three Years more; makes Thirty Six Years Purchase; the Value of the Land in Holland: And by the same Rule, interest being at six per cent in England, Land is worth but Twenty Years Purchase; and in Ireland, but Thirteen; Interest being there at Ten per cent: so that, according to the Rate of Interest, is that Value of the Land in the Country.

Therefore, Interest in all Countrys is setled by a Law, to make it certain; or else it could not be a Rule for the Merchant to make up his Account, nor the Gentleman, to Sell his Land by.

Of the Use and Benefit of Trade

The Use of Trade is to make, and provide things Necessary: Or useful for the Support, Defence, Ease, Pleasure, and Pomp of Life: Thus the Brewers, Bakers, Butchers, Poulterers, Cocks, with the

Apothecaries, Surgeons, and their Dependencies provide Food, and Medicine for the support of Life: the Cutlers, Gunsmiths, Powder- makers, with their Company of Traders, make things for Defence; The Shoo-makers Sadlers, Couch, and Chair-makers, with abundance more for the Ease of Life: The Perfumers, Fidlers, Painters, and Booksellers, and all those Trades that make things to gratifie the Sense, or delight the Mind, promote Pleasure: But those Trades that are imploy'd to express the Pomp of Life, are Infinite; for, besides those that adorn Mans Body, as the Glover, Hosier, Hatter, Semstriss, Taylor, and many more, with those that make the Materials to Deck it; as Clothier, Silk-Weaver, Lace-Maker, Ribbon-Weaver, with their Assistance of Drapers, Mercers, and Milliners, and a Thousand more: Those Trades that make the Equipage for Servants, Trappings for Horses; and those that Build, Furnish, and Adorn Houses, are innumerable.

Thus Busie Man is imployed, and it is for his own Benefit; For by Trade, the Natural Stock of the Country is improved, the Wool and Flax, are made into Cloth; the Skins, into Leather; and the Wood, Lead, Iron and Tin, wrought into Thousand useful Things: The Over-plus of these Wares not useful, are transported by the Merchants and Exchanged for the Wines, Oyls, Spices, and every Thing that is good of Forreign Countries: The Trader hath One Share for his Pains, and the Land-Lord the Other for his Rent: So, that by Trade, the Inhabitants in general, are not only well Fed, Clothed and Lodged; but the Richer sort are Furnished with all things to promote the Ease, Pleasure & Pomp of Life: Whereas, in the same Country, where there's no Trade, the Land-Lords would have but Coarse Diet, Coarser Clothes, and worse Lodgings; and nothing for the Rent of their Lands, but the Homage and Attendance of their Poor Bare-footed Tenants, for they have nothing else to give.

Trade Raiseth the Rent of the Land, for by the Use of several sorts of Improvements, the Land Yieldeth a greater natural Stock; by which, the Land-lord's Share is the greater: And it is the same thing, whether his Share be paid in Mony, or Goods; for the Mony must be laid out to Buy such Good's: Mony is an Immaginary Value made by a Law, for the Conveniency of Exchange: It is the Natural Stock that is the Real Value, and Rent of the Land.

Another Benefit of Trade, is, That, it doth not only bring Plenty, but hath occasioned Peace: For the Northern Nations, as they increased, were forced from the Necessities of their Climates, to Remove; and used to Destroy, and Conquer the Inhabitants of the Warmer Climates to make Room for themselves; thence was a Proverb, Omne Malum ab Aquilone: But those Northern People being settled in Trade, the Land by their Industry, is made more Fertile; and by the Exchange of the Nations Stock, for Wines and Spices, of Hotter Climates, those Countries become most Habitable; and the Inhabitants having Warmer Food, Clothes, and Lodgings, are better able to endure the Extreamitys of their Cold Seasons: This seems to be the Reason, that for these Seven or Eight Hundred years last past, there has been no such Invasions from the Northern part of the World, as used to destroy the Inhabitants of the Warmer Countries: Besides, Trade allows a better Price for labourers, than is paid for Fighting: So it is become more the Interest of Mankind to live at home in Peace, than to seek their fortunes abroad by Wars.

These are the Benefits of Trade, as they Relate to Mankind; those that Relate to Government, are many.

Trade Increaseth the Revenue of the Government, by providing an Imploy for the People: For every Man that Works, pay by those things which he Eats and Wears, something to the Government. Thus the Excise and Custom's are Raised, and the more every Man Earns, the more he Consumes, and the King's Revenue is the more Increased.

This shews the way of Determining those Controversies, about which sort of Goods are most beneficial to the Government, by their Making, or Importing: The sole difference is from the Number of hands imploy'd in making them; Hence the Importation of Raw Silk, is more Profitable to the Government than Gold, or Silver; Because there are more Hands imployd in the Throwing, and Weaving of the First; than there can be in working the Latter.

Another Benefit of Trade is, It is Useful for the Defence of the Government; It provides the Magazines of Warr. The Guns, Powder, and Bullets, are all made of Minerals, and are wrought by Traders; Besides, those Minerals are not to be had in all Countries; The great stock of Saltpeter is brought from the East Indies, and therefore must be Imported by the Merchant, for the Exchange of the Natives Stock.

The last Benefit is, That Trade may be Assistant to the Inlarging of Empire; and if an Universal Empire, or Dominion of very Large Extent, can again be raised in the World, It seems more probable to be done by the Help of Trade; By the Increase of Ships at Sea, than by Arms at land: This is too large a Subject to be here Treated of; but the French King's seeming Attempt to Raise Empire in Europe, being that Common Theam of Mens Discourse, has caused some short Reflections, which will appear by Comparing the Difficulty of the one, with the Probability of the other.

The Difficulties of Raising a Dominion of very Large Extent; especially in Europe, are Many.

First, Europe is grown more Populous than formerly,

and there are more Fortified Towns and Cities, than were in the time of the Roman Empire, which was the last extended Dominion; and therefore, not easily Subjected to the Power of any one Prince.

Whether Europe be grown more Populous, Solely by the Natural Increase of Mankind; There being more Born than Dye, which first Peopled the World?

Or, Whether, since the Inhabitants of Europe being Addicted to Trade, the ground is made more Fertile, and yields greater plenty of Food; which hath prevented famine, that formerly destroy'd great numbers of Mankind: So that no great Famines, has been taken Notice of by Historians, these Last Three Hundred Years?

Whether by Dreining Great Bogs, Lakes, and Fens, and Cutting down vast Woods, to make Room for the Increase of Mankind, the Air is Grown more Healthy; So that Plagues, and other Epidemical Diseases, are not so destructive as formerly? none so violent, as Procopius and Wallsingham Report, where destroyed such Vast Numbers in Italy, that there were not left Ten in a Thousand; and in other Parts of Europe, not enough alive to Bury the Dead. Whereas, the Plague in (1665) the Greatest since did not take away the Hundredth Person in England, Holland, and other Countries, where it Raged?

Whether, since the Invention of Guns and Gun-Powder, so many Men are not slain in the Wars as formerly? Xerxes lost 160000 in one Battle against the Grecians; Alexander destroyed 110000 of Darius's Army; Marius slew 120000 of the Cimbri; and in great Battles, seldome less than 100000 fell: but now 20000 Men are accounted very great Slaughter.

Whether, since the Northern People have fallen on Trade, such vast Numbers, are not destroyed by Invasions?

Whether, by all these Ways, or by which of them most, Europe is grown Populous, is not Material to this Discourse: It is sufficient to shew, that the Matter of Fact is so, which does appear by comparing the Antient Histories of Countries with the Modern?

In the Antient Descriptions, the Countries are full of Vast Woods, wild Beasts; the Inhabitants barbarous, and as wild, without Arts, and the Governments are like Colonies, or Herds of People: But in the Modern, the Woods are cut down, and the Lyons, Bears, and wild Beasts destroyed; no Flesh-Eaters are left to inhabit with man, but those Dogs and Cats that he tames for his Use: Corn grows where the Woods did, and with the Timber are built Cities, Towns and Villages; the People are cloathed, and have all Arts among them; and those little Colonies and Families, are increased into Great States and Kingdoms; and the most undeniable Proof of the Increase of Mankind in England, is the Doom-Day-Book, which was a Survey taken of all the Inhabitants of England, in the Reign of William the Conquerour; by which it appears, that the People of England are increased more than double since that time: But since the Mosaical Hypothesis of the Increase of the World, is generally believed amongst the Christians. And the late Lord Chief Justice Hales, in his Book of the Origination of Mankind, hath endeavoured to satisfie all the rest of the World. It would be misspending of time, to use any other Topick for the further Proof thereof, than what naturally follows in this Discourse, which is from the Different Success of Arms, in the Latter and Former Ages.

In the Infancy of the World, Governments began with little Families and Colonies of Men; so that, when ever any Government arrived to greater Heighth than the rest, either by the great Wisdom or Courage of the Government, they afterwards grew a pace: it was no Difficulty for Ninus, that was the oldest Government, and consequently, the most Populous, to begin the Assyrian Empire; nor for his Successors to continue and inlarge it: Such Vast Armies of Cyrus, Darius, Hystopis and Xerxes, the least of their Forces amounting to above 500000, could not be resisted, when the World was but thin Peopled.

These great Armies might at first sight, seem to infer, That the World was more Populous than now; because the Armies of the greatest Princes, seldom now exceed the Number of Fifty or Sixty Thousand Men; But the Reason of those great Numbers, was, They were not so well skilled in Military Arts, and shew that the World was in the Infancy of its Knowledge, rather than Populous; for all that were able to bear Arms, went to the Wars: And if that were now the Custom, there might be an Army in England of above Three Million, allowing the Inhabitants to be Seven Millions; and by the same Proportion, the King of France's Country, (being four times bigger) might raise Twelve Millions; such a Number was never heard of in this World.

The next Difficulty against the inlarging of Empire by Arms is, That since Printing, and the Use of the Needle hath been discovered, Navigation is better known, and thence is a Greater Commerce against Men, the Countries and Languages are more understood, Knowledge more dispersed, and the Arts of War in all Places known; so that, Men fight

more upon equal Terms than formerly; and like two Skilful Fencers, fight a long Time, before either gets Advantage.

The Assyrians & Persians Conquered more by the Number of Souldiers than Discipline; the Grecians and Romans, more by Discipline than Number; as the World grew older, it grew wiser: Learning first flourished among the Grecians, afterwards among the Romans; and as the Latter succeeded in Learning, so they did in Empire. But now both Parties are Equally Disciplin'd and Arm'd; and the Successes of War are not so great; victory is seldom gained without some Considerable Loss to the Conquerour.

Another Difficulty to the inlarging of Dominion by Arms, is, That the Goths overcoming the greatest part of Europe, did by their Form of Government, so settle Liberty, and Property of Land, that it is difficult for any Prince to Change that Form.

Whether the Goths were Part of the Ten Tribes, as some are of Opinion, and to Countenance their conjectures, have Compared the Languages of the Inhabitants, Wales, Finland and Orchadis, and other Northern Parts (little frequented by Strangers, which might alter their language) and find them to agree with the Hebrew in many Words and Sound, all their Speech being Guttural. This is certain, their Form of Government seems framed after the Examples of Moses's Government in the Land of Canaan, by dividing the Legislative Power, according to the Property of Land, according to that Antient Maxim, That Dominion is founded upon Property of Land. There Monarchy seems to be made by an easie Division of Land into Thirds, by a Conquering Army, setting down in Peace; the General being King, has one Third; the Colonels being the Lords, another Third; and the Captains, and other Inferiour Officers being Gentlemen, another; the Common Souldiers are the Farmers, and the Conquered are the Villains: The Legislative Power is divided amongst them, according to their Share in the Land; it being necessary that those that have Property of Land, should have Power to make Laws to Preserve it.

There seems to be but two settled Forms of government; the Turkish, and Gothick, or English Monarchy: They are both founded upon Property in Land; in the First, the Property and Legislative Power is solely in the Prince; In the Latter, they are in both the Prince and People: The one is best fitted to raise Dominion by Armies; for the Prince must be Absolute to give Command, according to the Various Fortunes of Warr: The other is Best for Trade; for men most industrious, where they are most free, and secure to injoy the Effects of their Labours.

All other Sorts of Government, either Aristocracy, or Democracy, where the Supream Magistrate is Elective, are Imperfect, Tumultuous, and Unsettled: For Man is Naturally Ambitious; he inherits the same Ruleing Spirit that God gave to Adam, to Govern the Creation with: And the oftener that the Throne is Empty, the oftener will Contentions and Struggles

31

Happen to get into it: Where deter digniori is the Rule, Warr always Ensues for the Golden Prize. Such Governments will never be without such Men as Marius and Scilla, to disturb them; nor without such a Man as Caesar to Usurp them; notwithstanding all the Contrivance for their Defence by those Polititians who seems fond of such Formes of Government.

The Gothick Government being a well fixed Form, and the People so free under it, is great hindedrance to the Enlarging of Dominion; for a People under a good Government do more Vigorously Defend it: A free People have more to lose than Slaves, and their Success is better Rewarded than by any Mercenary Pay, and therefore, make a better Resistance: It was the Freedom of the Grecians and Romans that raised their Courage, and had an equal Share in raising their Empires, with their Millitary Discipline: The free City of Tyre put Alexander to more Trouble to Conquer, than all the Citys of Asia.

The People of Asia, living under a Dispotick Power, made little Resistance; Alexander subdued Libia, Phoenicia, Pamphilia, without much Opposition in his Journey to meet Darius; Egypt came under Subjection without Fighting, and so did many Countries, being willing to Change the Persian Yoak: Besides, he Fought but two Battles for the whole Persian Empire; and the Resistance of those slavish People was so weak, that he did not lose 500 Grecians in either of the Battles, tho' Darius Number far exceeded his; the one being above 260000, and the other not Forty; And there was as great Disproportion in the Slaughter; for at the Battle in Cilicia he slew 110000, and that at Arbela 40000; whereas, the Spartan, a Free People, about the same time, fought with Antipater his Vice-Roy of Macedon; and in a Fight, where neither Army exceeded 60000, slew 1012 of the Macedonians, which was more than Alexander lost in both his Battles: so great is the difference of fighting against a Free, and a Slavish Effeminate People.

For the same Reasons, That the world is grown more

Populous, That the Arts of War are more known. That the People of Europe live under a Free Government. It is as difficult to keep a Country in Subjection, as to Conquer it. The People are too Numerous to be kept in Obedience: To destroy the greatest Part, were too Bloody, and Inhuman; To Burn the Towns, and Villages, and so force the People to remove, Is to lose the greatest share in conquest; for the People are the Riches and the Strength of the Country, And it is not much more Advantage to a Prince, to have a Title to Lands, in Terra Incognita, As to Countries without People.

Besides, Countries and Languages being more known; And Mankind more acquainted than formerly: The Oppressed People remove into the next Country they can find Shelter in, and become the Subjects of other Governments. By such Addition of Subjects, those Governments growing stronger, are better able to Resist the Incroaches of Empire: So that, every Conquest makes the next more difficult, from the Assistance of those People before Conquered; To Transplant the Conquered into a Remote Country, as formerly, Is not to be Practised; There is now no Room, the World is so full of People.

To Conquer, and leave them Free, only paying Tribute and Homage, Is the same as not to conquer them: For there is no Reason to expect their Submission longer, than till they are able to Resist; which will not be long before they make the same Opposition, if they continue in the same Possession; and therefore, though the Romans in the Infancy of their Government, did leave several Countries Free, as an Assistance to other Conquest; yet, when they grew stronger, they turned all their Conquest into Provinces, being the surest way to keep them from Revolting.

These are the Difficulties of inlarging Dominion at Land, but are not Impediments to its Rise at Sea: For those things that Obstruct the Growth of Empire at Land, do rather Promote its Growth at Sea. That the World is more Populous, is no Prejudice, there is Room enough upon the Sea; the many

Fortified Towns may hinder the March of an Army, but not the Sailing of Ships: The Arts of Navigation being discover'd, hath added an Unlimited Compass to the Naval Power. There needs no change of the Gothick Government; for that best Agrees with such an Empire.

The Ways of preserving Conquests gain'd by Sea, are different from those at Land. By the one, the Cities, Towns and Villages are burnt, to thin the People, that they may be the easier Governed, and kept into Subjection; by the other, the Cities must be inlarged, and New ones built: Instead of Banishing the People, they must be continued, in their Possession, or invited to the Seat of Empire; by the one, the Inhabitants are inslaved, by the other, they are made Free: The Seat of such an Empire must be in an Island, that their Defence may be solely in Shipping; the same way to defend their Dominion, as to inlarge it.

To conclude, there needs no other Argument, That Empire may be raised sooner at Sea, than at Land; than by observing the Growth of the United Provinces, within One Hundred Years last past, who have Changed their Style, from Poor Distressed, into that of High and Mighty States of the United Provinces: And Amsterdam, that was not long since, a poor Fisher-Town, is now one of the Chief Cities in Europe; and with the same compass of time, that the Spaniard & French have been endeavouring to Raise an Universal Empire upon the Land; they have risen to that Heighth, as to be an equal Match for either of them at Sea; and were their Government fitted for a Dominion of large Extent, and their country separated from their Troublesome Neighbour the Continent, which would Free them from that Military Charge in defending themselves, they might, in a short time, Contend for the Soveraignity of the Seats.

But England seems the Properer Seat for such an Empire: It is an Island, therefore requires no Military Force to defend it. Besides, Merchants and Souldiers never thrive in the same Place; It hath many large Harbours fitting for a large Dominion: The Inhabitants are naturally Couragious, as appears from the Effects of the Climate, in the Game Cocks, and Mastiff Dogs, being no where else so stout: The Monarchy is both fitted for Trade and Empire. And were there an Act for a General Naturalization, that all Forreigners, purchasing Land in England, might Enjoy the Freedom of Englishmen, It might within much less Compass of Time, than any Government by Arms at Land, arrive to such a Dominion: For since, in some Parts of Europe, Mankind is harrassed and disturbed with Wars; Since, some Governours have incroached upon the Rights fo their Subjects, and inslaved them; Since the People of England enjoy the Largest Freedoms, and Best government in the World; and since by Navigation and Letters, there is a great Commerce, and a General Acquaintance among Mankind, by which the Laws and Liberties of all Nations are known; those that are oppressed and inslaved, may probably Remove, and become the Subjects of England: And if the Subjects increase, the Ships, Excise and Customs, which are the Strength and Revenue of the Kingdom, will in Proportion increase, which may be so Great in a short Time, not only to preserve its Antient Soveraignty over the Narrow Seas, but to extent its Dominion over all the Great Ocean: an Empire, not less Glorious, and of a much larger Extent, than either Alexander's or Ceasar's.

Of the Chief Causes that Promote Trade

The Chief Causes that Promote Trade, (not to mention good Government, Peace, and Scituation, with other Advantages) are Industry in the Poor, and Liberality in the Rich: Liberality, is the free Usage of all those things that are made by the Industry of the Poor, for the Use of the Body and Mind; It Relates chiefly to Man's self, but doth not hinder him from being Liberal to others.

The Two Extreams to this Vertue, are Prodigality and Covetousness: Prodigality is a vice that is prejudicial to the Man, but not to Trade; It is living a pace, and spending that in a Year, that should last all his Life: Covetousness is a Vice, prejudicial both to Man and Trade; It starves the Man, and breaks the Trader; and by the same way the Covetous Man thinks he grows rich, he grows poor; for by not consuming the goods that are provided for Man's Use, there ariseth a dead Stock, called Plenty, and the Value of those goods fall, and the Covetous Man's Estates, whether in Land, or Mony, become less worth: And a Conspiracy of the Rich Men to be Covetous, and not spend, would be as dangerous to a Trading State, as a Forreign War; for though they themselves get nothing by their Covetousness, nor grow the Richer, yet they would make the Nation poor, and the government great Losers in the Customs and Excises that ariseth from Expence.

Liberality ought chiefly to be Excercised in an equal Division of the Expence amongst those things that relate to Food, Cloaths, and Lodging; according to the Portion, or Station, that is allotted to every Man, with some allowance for the more refined Pleasures of the Mind; with such Distributions, as may please both sect of Philosophers, Platonist and Epicureans: The Belly must not be starved to cloath the Back-Part.

Those Expences that most Promote Trade, are in Cloaths

and Lodging: In Adorning the Body and the House, There are a Thousand Traders Imploy'd in providing Food. Belonging to Cloaths, is Fashion; which is the shape or Form of Apparel.

In some places, it is fixt and certain; as all over Asia, and in Spain; but in France, England, and other places, the Dress alters; Fashion or the alteration of Dress, is a great Promoter of Trade, because it occasions the Expence of Cloaths, before the Old ones are worn out: It is the Spirit and Life of Trade; It makes a Circulation, and gives a Value by Turns, to all sorts of Commodities; keeps the great Body of Trade in Motion; it is an Invention to Dress a Man, as if he lived in a perpetual Spring; he never sees the Autum of his Cloaths: The following of the Fashion, Is a Respect paid to the Prince and his Court, by approving his Choice in the shape of Dress. It lyes under an ill Name amongst many Grave and Sober People, but without any Just Cause; for those that Exclaim against the Vanity of the New Fashion, and at the same time, commend that Decency of the Old one, forget that every Old Fashion was once New, and then the same Argument might have been used against it. And if an Indian, or Stranger, that nvever saw any person Cloathed before, were to be Judge of the Controversy, and were to Determin upon seeing at the same time a well Drest-Courtier in the New Fashion, and another in the Old, which is accounted Decent; and a third in the Robes of an Officer, which by common Esteem, had a Reverence: It will be Two to One, against any One of the Grave Fashions; for it's only Use and Custom by which Habits become Grave and Decent, and not any particular Conveniency in the shape; for if Conveniency were the Rule of Commendation, Whether the Spanish garb made strait to the Body, or the loose Habit of the Turks, were to be Chosen? And therefore since all Habits are equally handsome, and hard to know which is most Convenient: The Promoting of New Fashions, ought to be Encouraged, because it provides a Livelihood for a great Part of Mankind.

The next Expence that chiefly promotes Trade, is Building, which is natural to Mankind, being the making of a

Nest or Place for his Birth, it is the most proper and vible Distinction of Riches, and Greatness; because the Expences are too Great for Mean Persons to follow. It is a Pleasure fit to entertain Princes; for a Magnificient Structure doth best represent the Majesty of the Person that lives init, and is the most lasting and truest History of the Greatness of his Person.

Building is the chiefest Promoter of Trade; it Imploys a greater Number of Trades and People, than Feeding or Cloathing: the Artificers that belong to building, such as Bricklayers, Carpenters, Plaisterers, etc. imploy many Hands; Those that make the Materials for Building, usch as Bricks, Lyme, Tyle, etc. imploy more; and with those that Furnish the Houses, such as Upholsterers, Pewterers, etc. they are almost Innumerable.

In Holland, where Trade hath made the Inhabitants very Rich, It is the Care of the government, to Incourage the Builder, and at the Charge of the State, the Grafts and Streets are made. And at Amsterdam, they have three times, at great Expence, Thrown down the walls of thier City, and Dreined the Boggs, to make Room for the Builder: For Houses are the Places where the Artificers make their Goods, and Merchants Sell them; and without New Houses, the Trades and Inhabitants could not Increase.

Beside, There is another great Advantage to Trade, by Enlarging of cities; the Two Beneficial Expences of cloathing and Lodging, are Increased; Man being Naturally Ambitious, the Living together, occasion Emulation, which is seen by Out-Vying one another in Apparel, Equipage, and Furniture of the House; whereas, if a Man lived Solitary alone, his chiefest Expence, would be Food. It is from this very Custom; If the Gentry of France Living in Cities, with the Invention of Fashion; that France, tho' a Country no way fitted for Trade, has so great a share of it: It is from Fashion in Cloaths, and Living in Cities, that the King of France's Revenues is so great, by which he is become troublesome to his Neighbours, and will always be so, while he can preserve Peace within his own Country; by which, those Fountains of riches, may run Interrupted into his Exchequer.

Of the Chief Causes of the Decay of Trade in England, and Fall of the Rents of Land

The Two Chief Causes of the Decay of Trade, are the many Prohibitions and high Interest.

The Prohibition of Trade, is the Cause of its Decay; for all Forreign Wares are brought in by the Exchange of the Native: So that the Prohibiting of any Foreign Commodity, doth hinder the Making and Exportation of so much of the Native, as used to be Made and Exchanged

for it. The Artificiers and Merchants, that Dealt in such Goods, lose their Trades; and the Profit that was gained by such Trades,and laid out amongst other Traders, is Lost. The Native Stock for want of such Exportation, Falls in Value, and the Rent of the Land must Fall with the Value of the Stock.

The common Argument for the Prohibiting Foreign Commodities, is, That the Bringing in, and Consuming such Forreign Wares, hinders the Making and Consuming the like sort of Goods of our own Native Make and Growth; therefore Flanders-Lace, French-Hats, Gloves, Silks, Westphalia-Bacon, etc. are Prohibited, because it is supposed, they hinder the Consumption of English Lace, Gloves, Hats, Silk, Bacon, etc. But this is mistaken Reason, and ariseth by not considering what it is that Occasions Trade. It is not Necessity that causeth the Consumption, Nature may be Satisfied with little; but it is the wants of the Mind, Fashion, and desire of Novelties and things scarce, that causeth Trade. A Person may have English-Lace, Gloves, or Silk, as much as he wants, and will Buy no more such; and yet, lay out his Mony on a Point of Venice, Jessimine-Gloves, or French-Silks; he may desire to Eat Westphalia-Bacon, when he will not English; so that, the Prohibition of Forreign Wares, does not necessarily cause a greater Consumption of the like sort of English.

Besides, There is the same wants of the Mind in Foreigners, as in the English; they desire Novelties; they Value English-cloth, Hats, and Gloves, and Foreign Goods, more than their Native make; so that, tho' the Wearing or Consuming of Forreign Things, might lessen the consuming of the same sort in England; yet there may not be a lesser Quantity made; and if the same Quantity be make, it will be a greater Advantange to the Nation, if they Consumed in Foreign Countries, than at home; because the Charge, and Imploy of the Freight, is Gained by it, which in bulky Goods, may be a Fourth Part of the whole Value.

The particular Trades that expect an Advantage by such Prohibition, are often mistaken; For if the Use of most Commodities depending upon Fashion, which often alters; the Use of those Goods cease. As to Instance, Suppose a Law to Prohibit Cane-Chairs, (which are already in use amongst the Gentry, The Cane-Chairs being grown too Cheap and Common) or else, they may lay aside the Use of all Chairs, Introducing the Custom of Lying upon Carpets; the Ancient Roman Fashion; still in Use amongst the Turks, Persians, and all the Eastern Princes.

Lastly, If the Suppressing or Prohibiting of some sorts of Goods, should prove an Advantage to the Trader, and Increase the Consumption of the same sort of our Native Commodity: Yet it may prove a Loss to the Nation. for the Advantage to the Nation from Trade, is, from the Customs, and from those Goods that Imploys most Hands. So that, tho' the Prohibition may Increase, as the Consumption of the like sort of the Native; yet if it should Obstruct the Transporting of other goods which were Exchanged for them, that Paid more custom, Freight, or Imployed more Hands in making; the Nation will be a loser by the Prohibition: As to Instance, If Tobacco or Woollen-Cloth were used to Exchange for Westphaly-Bacon, The Nation loseth by the Prohibition, tho' it should Increase the Consumption of English-Bacon; because the First, Pays more Freight and

Custom; and the Latter, Imploys more Hands. By this Rule it appears, That the Prohibiting of all unwrought Goods, such as raw Silk, Cotton, Flax, etc. and all Bulky goods; such as Wines, Oyls, Fruits, etc. would be a Loss to the Nation; because nothing can be sent in Exchange that Imploys fewer Hands than the First, or Pays greater Freight than the Latter.

But all Trading Countries Study their Advantage of Trade, and Know the difference of the Profit by the Exchange of wrought Goods, for unwrought: And therefore, for any Nation to make a Law to Prohibit all Foreign Goods, but such only as are most Advantageous; Is to put other Nations upon making the same Laws; and the Consequence will be to Ruine all Foreign Trade. For the Foundation of all Forreign Trade, is, from the Exchange of the Native Commodities of each Country, for one another.

To Conclude, If the bringing in of Foreign Goods, should hinder the making and consuming of the Native, which will very seldom happen; this disadvantage is not to be Remedied by a Prohibition of those Goods; but by Laying so great Duties upon them, that they may be always Dearer than those of our Country make: The Dearness will hinder the common Consumption of them, and preserve them for the Use of the Gentry, who may Esteem them, because they are Dear; and perhaps, might not Consume more of the English Growth, were the other not Imported. By such duties, the Revenue of the Crown, will be increased; and no Exceptions can be taken by any Foreign Prince or Government; Since it is in the Liberty of every Government, to lay what Duty or Imposition they please. Trade will continue Open, and Free; and the Traders, Enjoy the Profit of their Trade: The Dead Stock of the Nation, that is more than can be Used, will be carried off, which will keep up the Price of the Native Stock, and the Rent of the Land.

The next cause of the Decay of Trade in England, and the Fall of Rents, is, That Interest is higher in England, than in Holland, and other places of great Trade: It is at Six per cent in

England and at Three in Holland; For all Merchants that Trade in the same sort of Goods, to the same Ports, should Trade by the same Interest.

Interest is the Rule of buying and Selling: And being higher in England, than in Holland; the English Merchant Trades with a Disadvantage, because he cannot Sell the same sort of Goods in the same Port, for the same Value as the Dutch Merchant. The Dutch Merchant can Sell 100 l. worth of Goods, for 103 l. And the English Merchant must Sell the same sort, for 106 l. to make the same Account of Principal and Interest.

Besides, And the English Merchant hath the same Disadvantage in the Return of the Goods he buys; for the Dutch Merchant making his Return in the same sort of Goods, can under-Sell him.

By this Difference of Interest, Holland is become to be the great Magazine, and Store-House of this Part of Europe, for all sorts of Goods: For they may be laid up cheaper in Holland, than in England.

It is impossible for the Merchant when he has Bought his goods, To know what he shall sell them for: The Value of them, depends upon the Difference betwixt the Occasion and the Quantity; tho' that be the Chiefest of the Merchants Care to observe, yet it depends upon so many Circumstances, that it's impossible to know it. Therefore if the plenty of the goods,has brought down the Price; the Merchant layeth them up, till the Quantity is consumed, and the Price riseth. But the English Merchant, cannot lay up his, but with Disadvantage; for by that time, the Price is risen so as to pay Charges and Interest at Six per cent the same Goods are sent for from Holland, and bring down the

Price: For they are laid up there, at three per cent and can therefoer be sold cheaper.

For want of Considering this, in England, many an English Merchant has been undone; for, though by observing the Bill of Lading, he was able to make some Guess of the Stock that was Imported here; and therefore, hath kept his Goods by him for a Rise: But not knowing what Stock there was in Holland, hath not been able to sell his Goods to Profit, the same Goods being brought from thence before the Price riseth high enough to pay Ware-House-Room, and Interest.

So that, now the great part of the English Trade is driven by a quick Return, every Day Buying and Selling, according to a Bill of Rate every day Printed. By this Means, the English Trade is narrowed and confined, and the King loseth the Revenue of Importation, which he would have, if England were the Magazine of Europe; and the Nation loseth the Profit, which would arise from the Hands imploy'd in Freight and Shipping.

Interest being so high in England, is the Cause of the Fall of Rents; for Trade being confined to a Quick Return: And the Merchant being not able to lay up Foreign Goods, at the same Interest as in Holland, he Exports less of the Native; and the Plenty of the Native Stock Brings down the Rent of Land; for the rest of the Land that produceth the Stock, must fall, as the Price of the Stock doth.

Whereas, if Interest were at the same Rates as in Holland, at Three per cent it would make the Rent more certain, and raise the Value of the Land.

This Difference of Three per cent is so Considerable, that many Dutch Merchants Living in Holland, having Sold their Goods in England; give order, to put out their Stock to Interest in England; thinking That a better Advantage than they can make by Trade.

It will raise the Rent of some Estates, and preserve the Rent of others: For the Farmer must make up his Account, as the Merchant doth; the Interest of the Stock, must be reckoned, as well as the Rent of Land: Now if the Farmer hath 300 l. Stock, upon his Farm, that is so easily Rented, that he lives well upon it; he may add 9 l. per annum more to the rent, when the interest is at three per cent and make the same Account of Profit from the Farm: As he doth now Interest , is at six per cent. And those Farmers that are hard rented, having the same stock, will have 9 l. per annum Advance in the Account, towards the Easing the Rent: Fro altho' the Farmer gets nothing more at the Years end, yet in making up of Account, towards the Easing the Rent: For altho' the Farmer gets nothing more at the Years end, yet in making up of Account, there must 9 l. add to the Value of Land, and taken from the Account of the Stock. If Interest were at Three per cent there would always be a Magazine of Corn and Wooll in England,which would be agrat Advantage to the Farmer, and make his Rent more certain; for there are Years of Plenty, and Scarcity; and there are more Farmers undone by Years of great Plenty, than Recover themselves in Years of Scarcity; for when the Price is very low, the Crop doth not pay the Charge of Sowing, Farming, and Carrying to Market; and when it is Dear, It doth not fall to all Mens fortune that were losers by Plenty, to have a Crop: Now if Interest were at three per cent Corn and Wooll in Years of great Plenty, would be Bought and Laid up to be Sold in Years of Scarcity. The Buying in Years of Plenty, would keep the Price from Falling too low; and the Selling in Years of Scarcity, would prevent it from Rising too High; by this means, a moderate Price, being best upon Corn and Wooll; the Farmers Stock and Rent of Land, would be more certain.

But now Holland being the great Magazine of Corn, Man will Lay up any considerable Quantity in England at Six per cent when he may always Buy as much as he wants, that was Laid up at Three per cent and may bring it from thence, as soon, and as Cheap, into any Parts of England, as if it were laid up here.

Thirdly, If Interest were at Three per cent the Land of England, would be worth from Thirty six, to Forty Years Purchase; for Interest, sets the Price in the Buying and Selling of Land.

The bringing down of Interest, will not alter the Value of other Wares; for the Value of all Wares, arriveth from their Use; and the Dearness and Cheapness of them, from their Plenty and Scarcity: Nor will it make Mony more Scarce. For if the Law allow no more Interest, than Three per cent they that live upon it, must Lend at that rate, or have no Interest; for they cannot put it forth any where else to better Advantage. but if it be supposed, that it may make Mony scarce, and that it may be a Prejudice to the Government, who want the Advance of the Mony; It may be provided for, by a Clause, that all that Lend Mony to the King, shall have 6 l. per cent; such Advantage would make all Men lend to the Government: And the King will save two per cent by such a law.

The seeming Prejudice from such a law, is, It will lessen the Revenue of those who live upon Interest: But this will not be a General Prejudice; for many of those Persons have Land as well as Mony, and will get as much by the Rise of one, as the fall of the other. Besides, many of them, are Persons that live Thriftily, and much within the Compass of their Estates; and therefore, will not want it, but in Opinion. they have had a long Time, the Advantage of the Borrower; for the Land yielding but 4 l. per cent and the Interest being at 6 l. per cent a new Debt is every Year contracted of 2 l. per cent more than the Value of the Debt in Land will pay, which hath Devoured many a good Farm; and eat up the Estates of many of the Ancient Gentry of England.

Moses, that Wise Law-Giver, who designed, that the Land divided amongst the Jews, should continue in their Families; forbid the Jews to pay Interest, well knowing that the Merchants of Tyre, who were to be their near Neighbours, would, by Lending Mony at Interest, at last get their Lands: And that this seems to be the Reason, is plain; For the Jews might take Interest of Strangers, but not pay; for by taking Interest, they could not lose their Estates.

The Lawyers have invented Intails, to preserve Estates

in Families; and the bringing down of Interest to three per cent will much help to continue it; because the Estates being raised to double the Value, will require double the time, after the same Proportion of Expence to Consume it in.

The raising the Value of Land, at this Time, seems most necessary, when the Nation is Engages in such a Chargeable War: For the Land is the Fund that must support and preserve the Government; and the Taxes will be lesser and easier payd; for they will not be so great: For 3 sh. in the Pound, is now 133 1/2 Part of every Mans Estate in Land, reckoning at Twenty Years Purchase. But if the Value of the Land be doubled, it will be the 226 Part of the Land,which may be much easier born.

Campinella, who Wrote an 100 years since, upon considering of the great Tract of the Land of France; says, That if ever it were United under one Prince, it would produce so great a Revenue; it might give Law to all Europe.

The Effect of this Calculation, Is since, seen by the Attempts of this present King of France: And therefore, since England is an Island, and the Number of Acres cannot be Increased; It seems absolutely necessary, That the Value of them, should be raised to Defend the nation against such a Powerful Force: It will be some Recompence to the Gentry, whose Lands must bear the Burthen of the War, to have the Value of their Estates Raised; which is the Fund and Support of the Government; Is a great Advantage to the whole Nation; and its the greater, because it doth not Disturb, Lessen, nor Alter the Value of any Thing else.

FINIS.

Publisher's Note

This book was written in 1690, and thus utilized typography, words and writing styles that are not common today. It's presented here in its original form to preserve historical accuracy.

Also available from the publisher:

Principles of Philosophy of the Future – Ludwig Feuerbach

How the Gods were Made – John Keracher

Selected Works of Salvador Allende

Ethics of Socialism – Ernest Belfort Bax

Twenty Years in Underground Russia – Cecilia Bobrovskaya

The Decline of American Capitalism – Lewis Corey

Imperialism and the Revolution – Enver Hoxha

The Selected Works of Kim Il Sung

The Stalin Era – Anna Louise Strong

www.PrismKeyPress.com